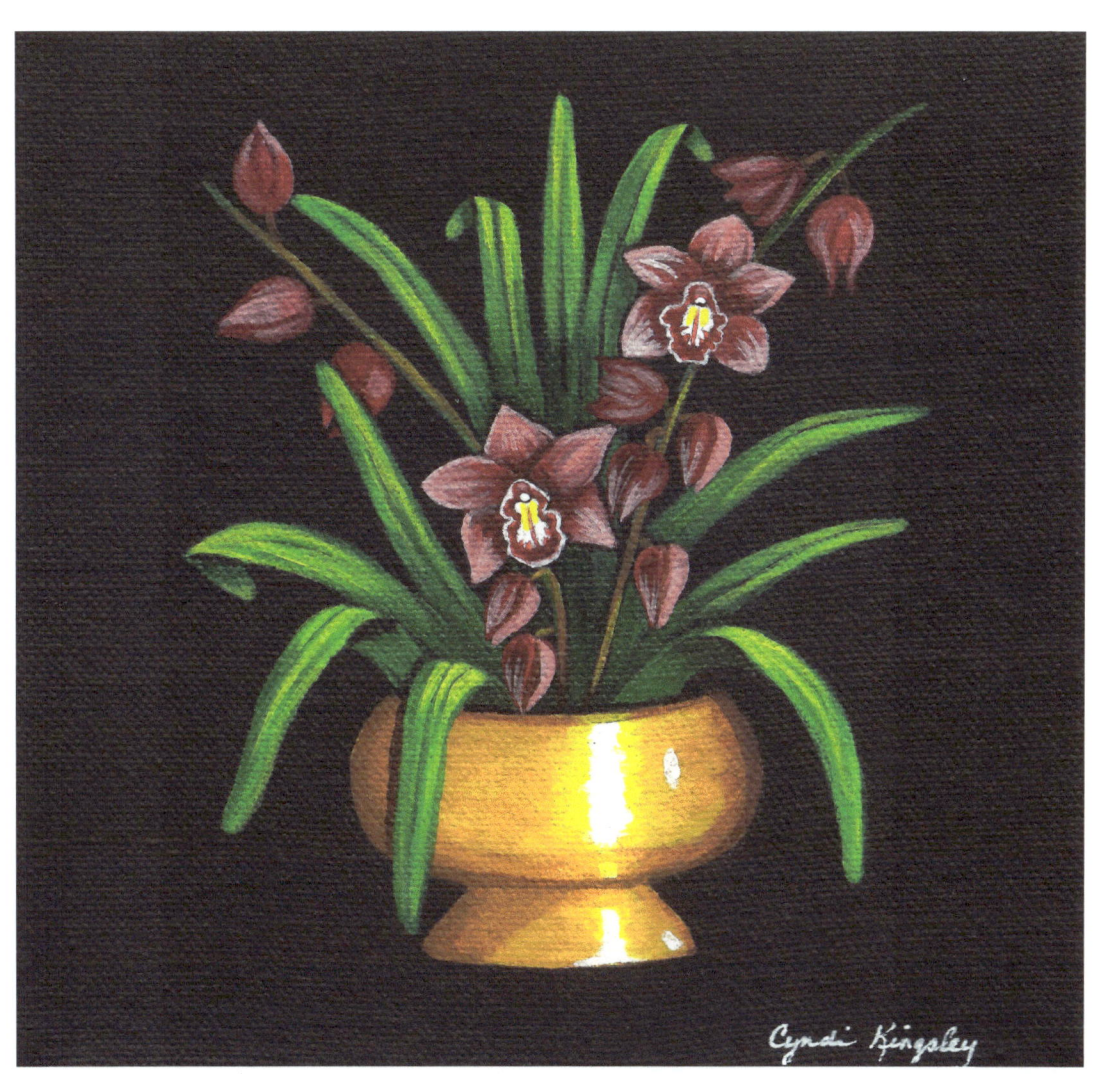

Text copyright 2022 Cyndi Kingsley
Illustrations copyright 2022 Cyndi Kingsley

All rights reserved. No part of this publication may be reproduced in any way, shape, or form.

THE ARTWORK OF CYNDI KINGSLEY

VOLUME I

I grew up in Rochester, New York where lilacs grow prolifically. Almost every yard has lilacs blooming and they grow in every shade of purple. Their intoxicating smell is beautiful. I was happy to sell this painting to a woman who swore she could smell the lilacs when she looked at the painting.

In the month of May, since the late 1800s, Rochester has annually held the world famous Lilac Festival.

ARRANGING THE LILACS
acrylics with brush on card stock
original painting-9" x 12"

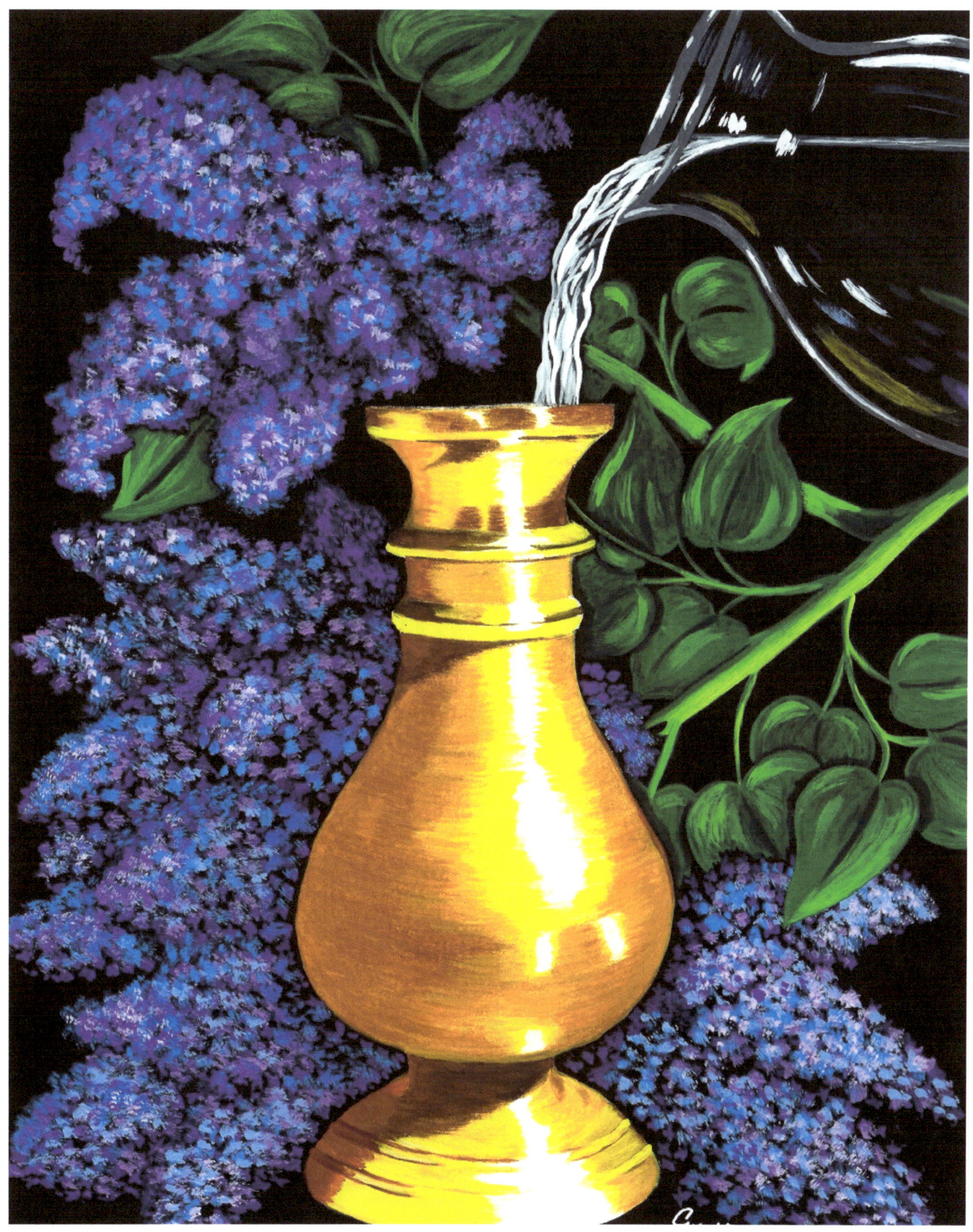

Often, I will paint places I would like to visit. This lighthouse is one of those places. Painting from a photograph, I was able to put down, on canvas, this beautiful Hawaiian paradise.

Lighthouse
Makapuu Point-Hawaii
acrylics with brush on canvas
original painting- 9 " x 12"

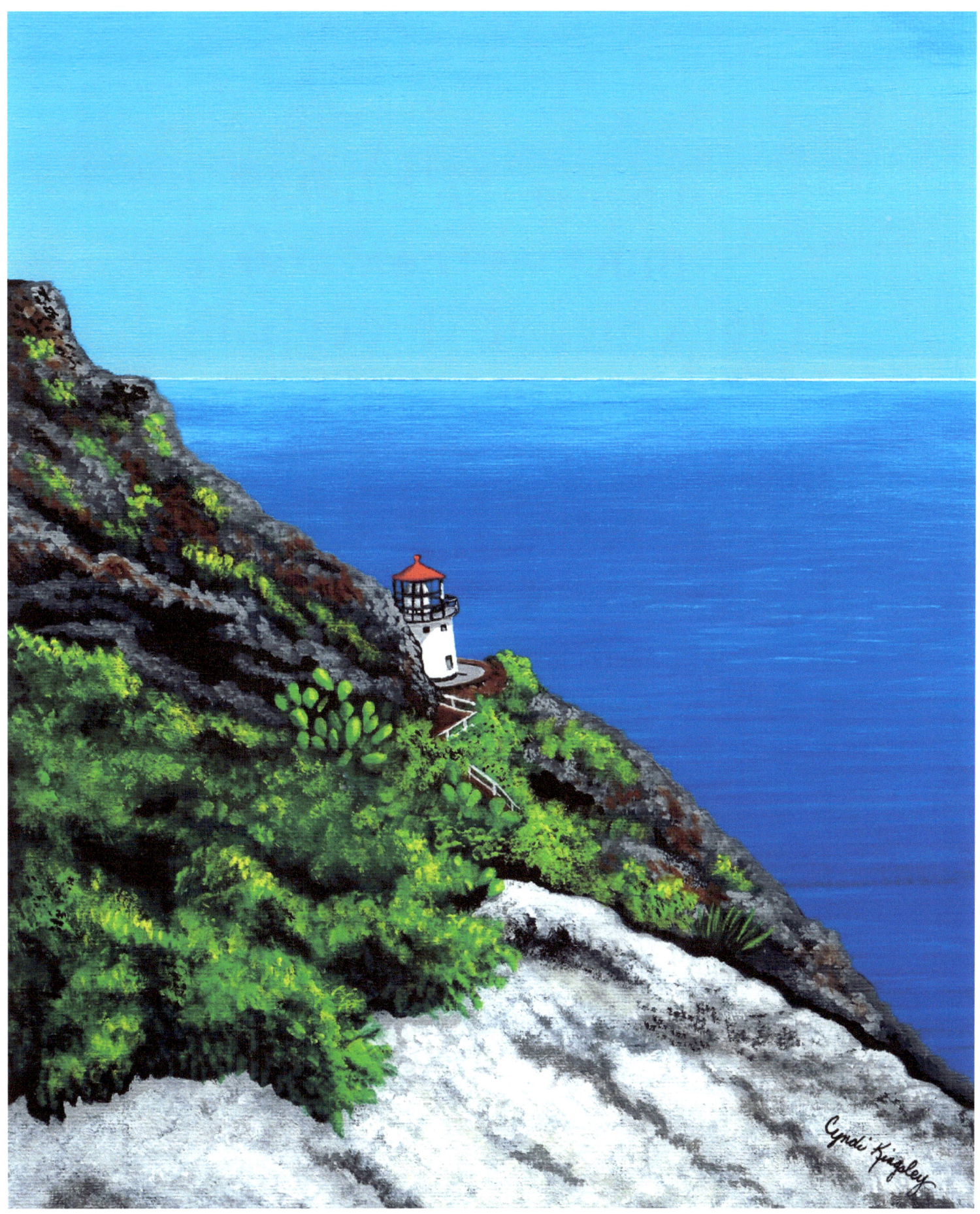

Loving the jungle as much as the water, I took myself, through my imagination and paint brush, to a place where exotic birds fly and maybe, just maybe, Tarzan might swing by to say, "Hi".

Jungle and Toucan
acrylics with brush on canvas
Original painting- 9" x 12"

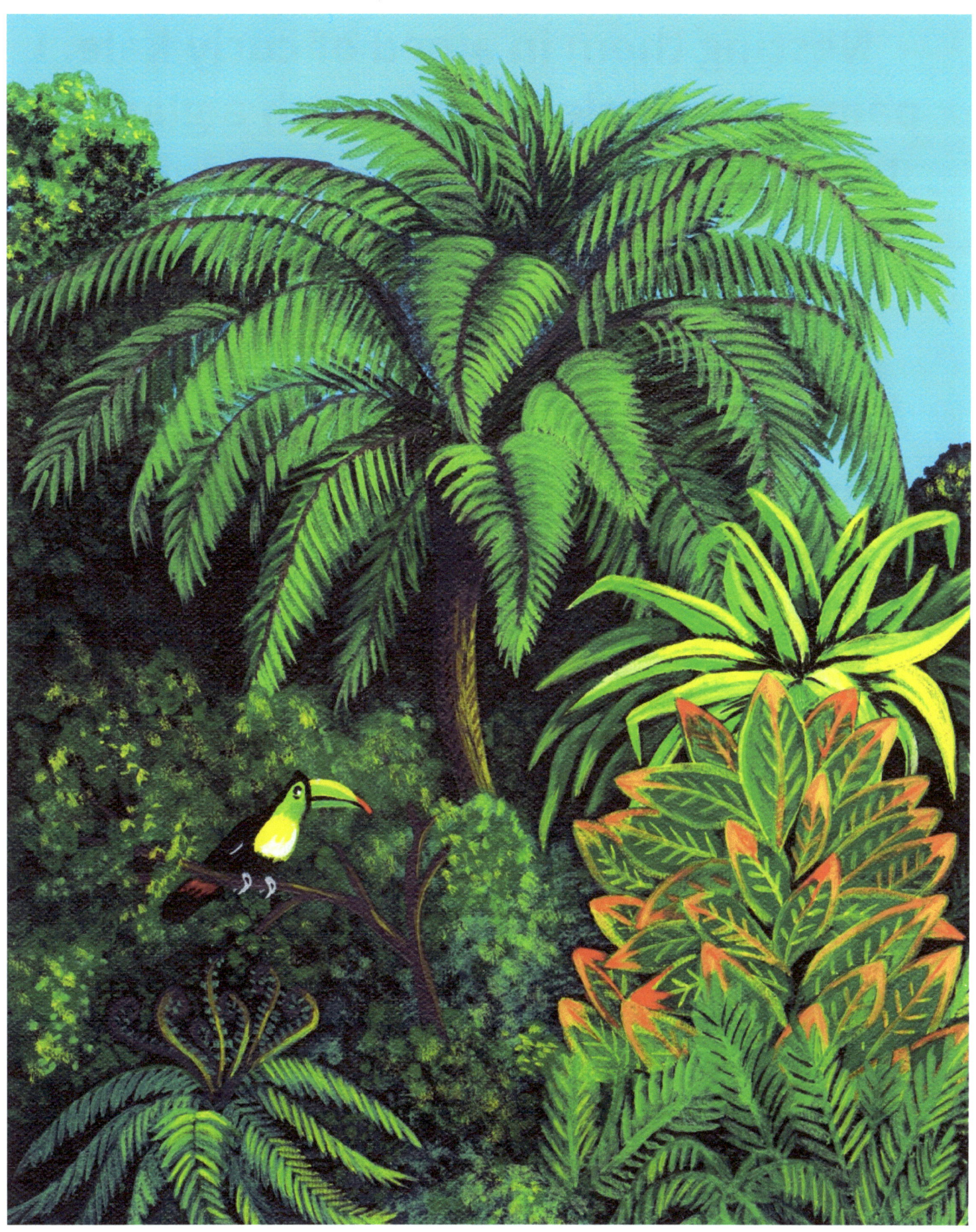

Nesting them in a bed of curly kale, I painted a bottle of wine with a glass. As I looked at the painting, my imagination took off and I added more and more of the foods I liked.

Mushrooms, lobster, mini croissant, cheese, shrimp, jalapeno peppers, chili peppers, carrot, avocado, cherry tomatoes, lemon, sausage, asparagus, grapes, garlic, scallions, red onion, and yellow squash, all made the painting into a
"Fabulous Feast".

Fabulous Feast
acrylics with brush on canvas
original painting- 9" x 12"

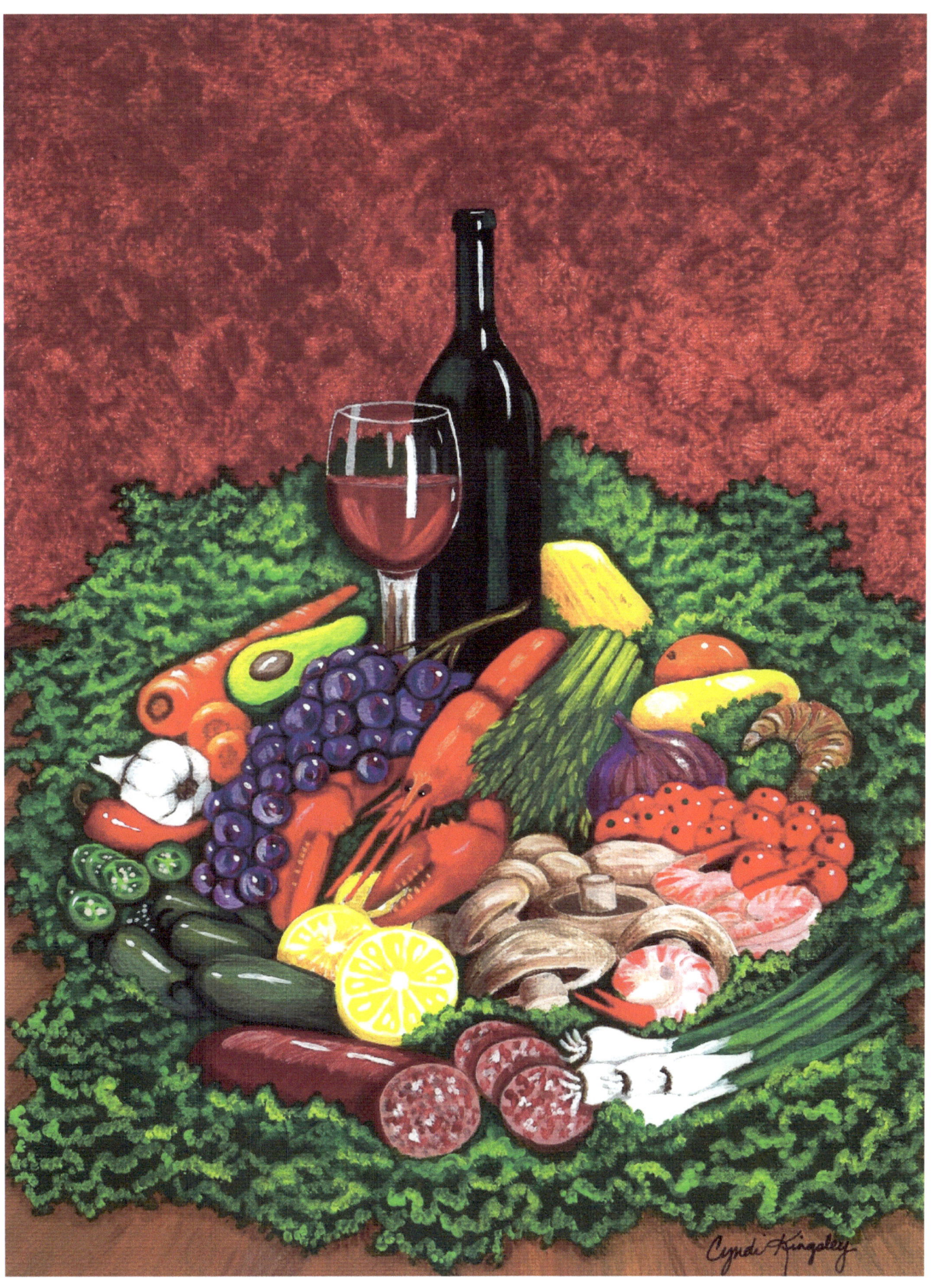

My adult niece loves to bake. A few years back, she shared a photo of the ingredients she was using to make a cake. I was so impressed by the stacked up egg shells, (seriously, her stack of shells was that high) that my mind started to imagine my own version of that scene and I went to work, with brush and paint, on "Getting Ready To Bake". A Copper bowl, flour, milk, butter, honey, strawberries, egg carton and wooden spoon make up this painting.

Getting Ready To Bake
acrylics with brush on canvas
original painting- 9" x 12"

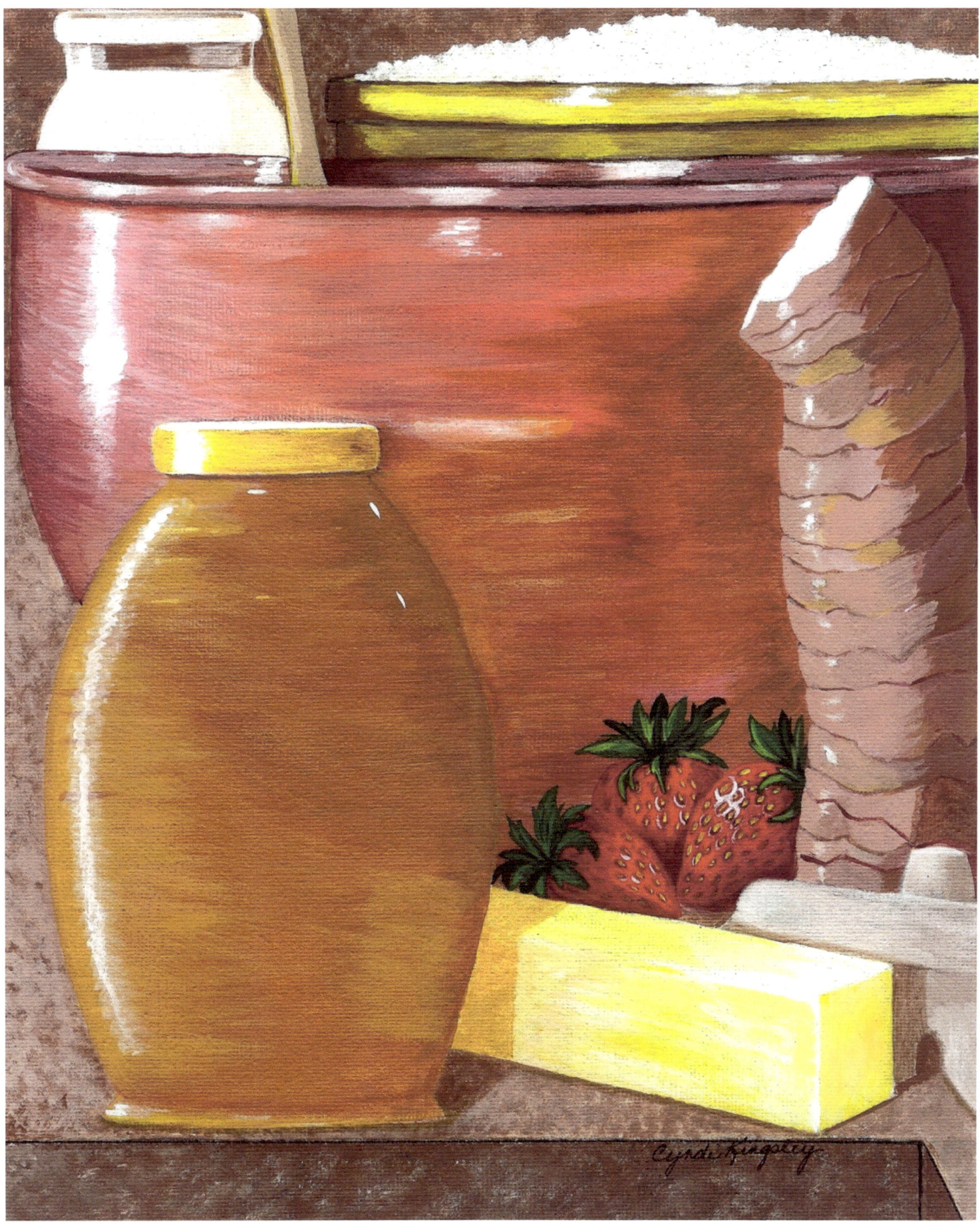

At one time, I belonged to an online art website where they often had contests. Different theme challenges were put into place for the individual artists to participate.
"High Heel Sneakers" was my entry into the challenge of painting a picture containing "shoes".
I didn't win the contest, where fellow artists did the voting, but still had fun painting the subject.

High Heel Denim Sneakers acrylics with brush on canvas original painting-9" x 12"

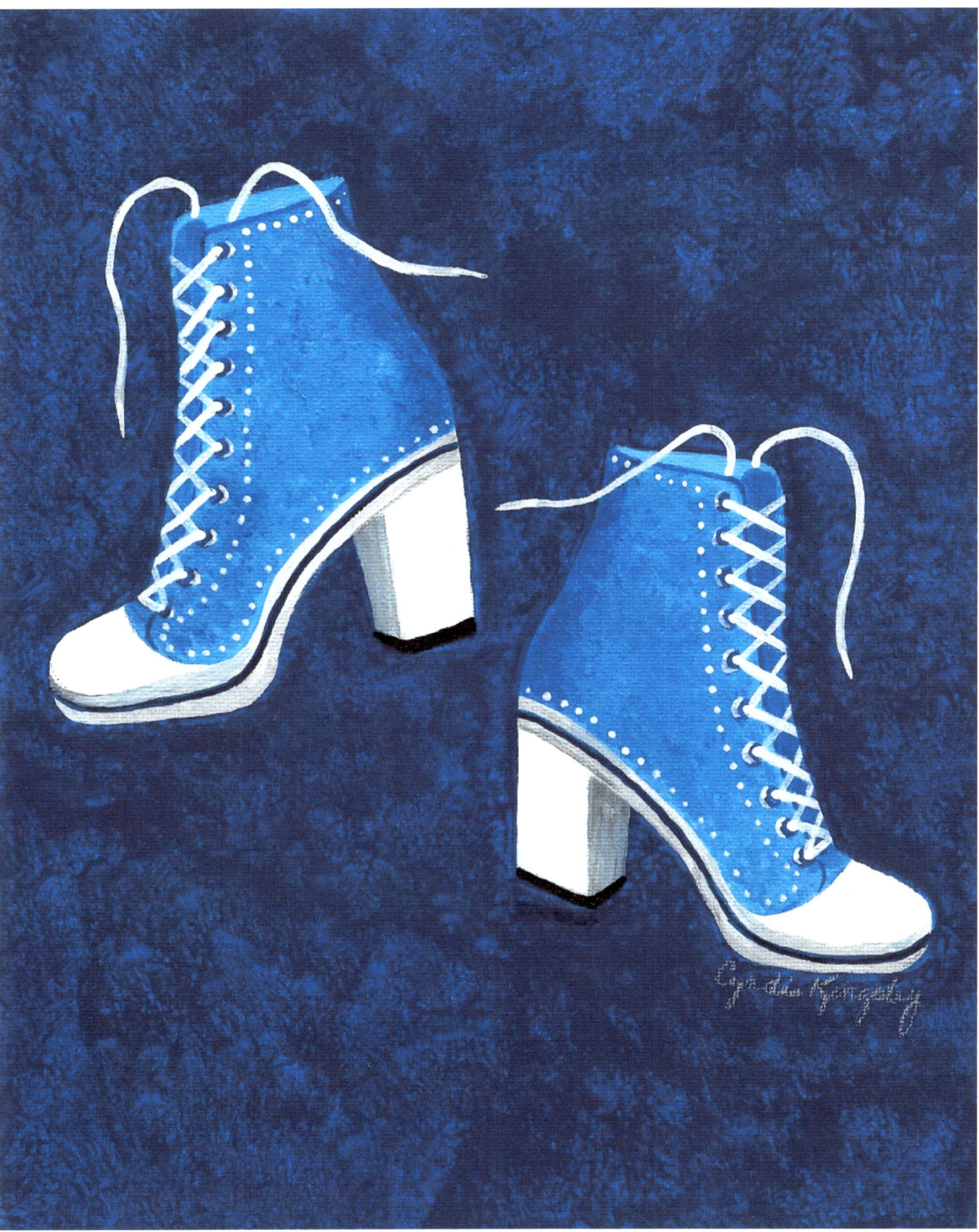

During an art contest, I took on the challenge of the subject, "cherries".
Cherries had to be incorporated, in some way, into the painting.
My submission won first prize.

Cherries in Wine Glass
acrylics with brush on cardstock
original painting- 9" x 12"

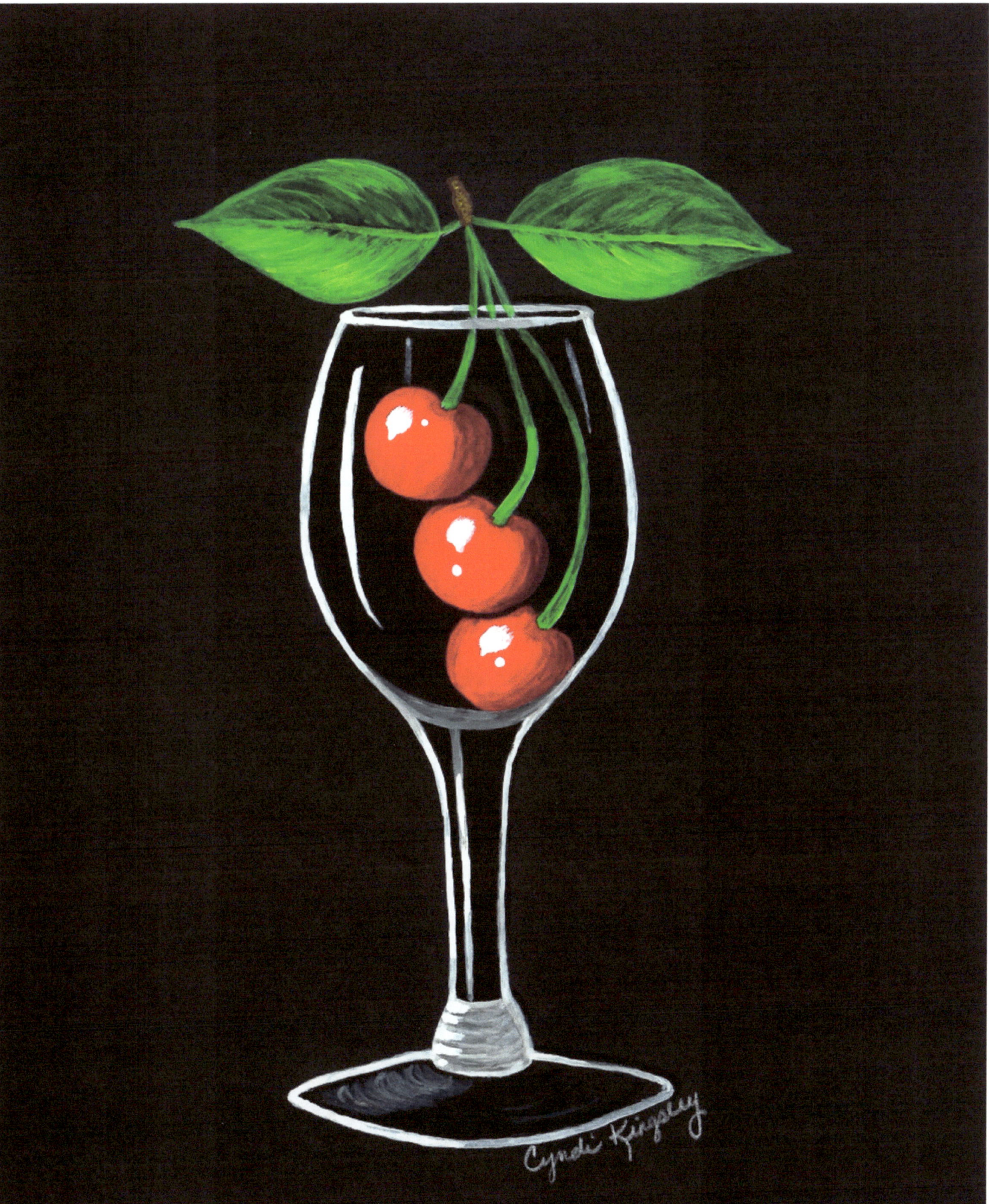

My wonderful niece loves my artwork. I love her knitting. She asked me to paint her a picture of strawberries and cream. I asked her to knit a sweater for my Poodle, Max. And that's how "Strawberries and Cream" came to be. It was a bartering of talents.

Strawberries and Cream
acrylics with brush on canvas
original painting- 9" x 12"

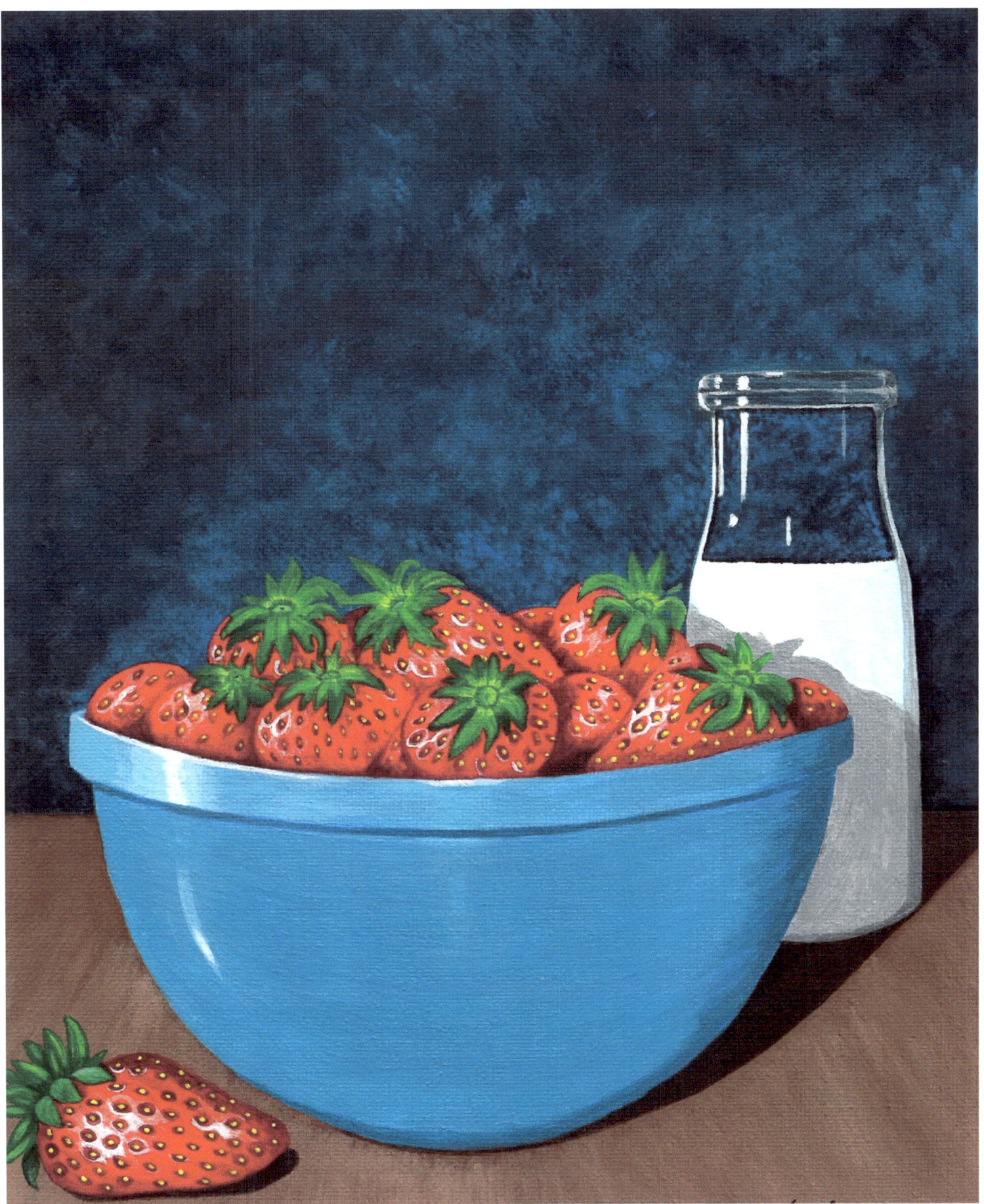

One of my sons follows a vegan lifestyle of eating, and so, loves vegetables in any way shape or form. This painting of "Celery And Peppers" was painted for him as a Christmas gift. He can't eat *these painted vegetables,* but he sure likes looking at them.

Celery and Peppers
acrylics with brush on canvas
original painting- 8" x 10"

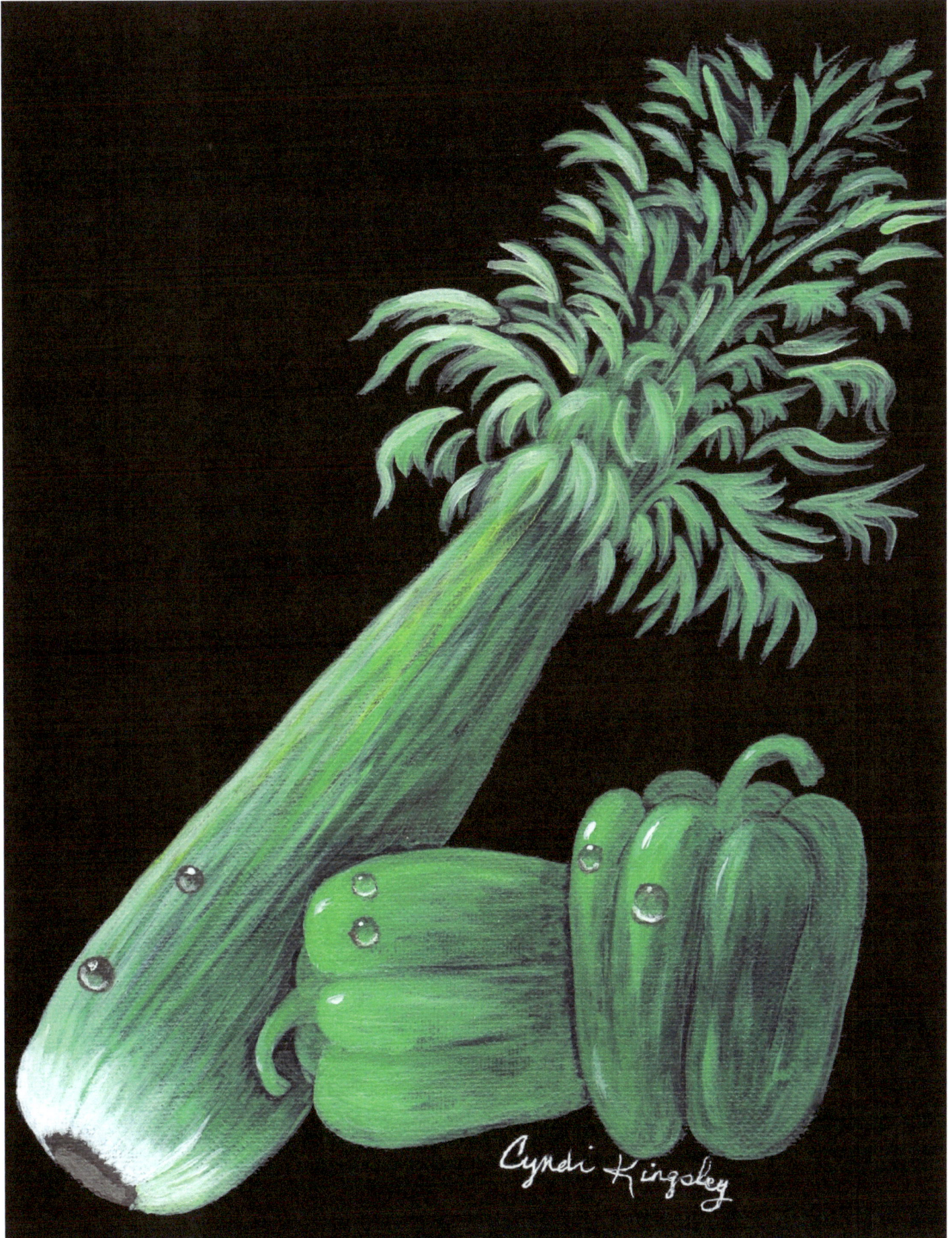

I thought I'd try my hand at drawing with colored pencils. It took some getting used to, but finally got a feel for it. I love, and grow, orchids so I used them for my subject. The "White Orchid" is the first of three different orchids that I did.

White Orchid
colored pencil on black card stock
original-9" x 12"

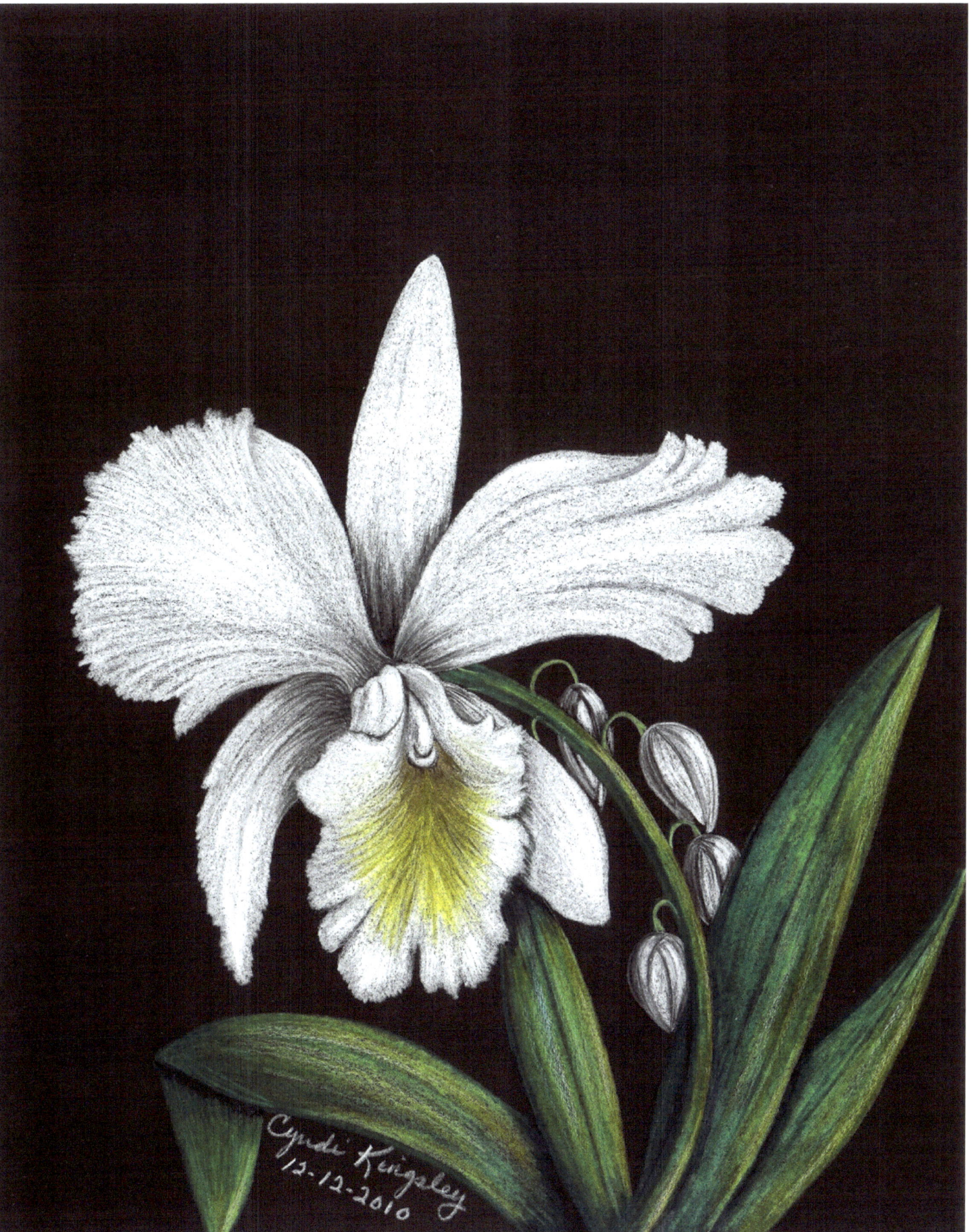

This orchid was the second orchid I did. I found that working with colored pencils allowed for greater control of details than I have working with paint. BUT, I also found that colored pencils are far less forgiving than paints. Some artists may argue about this point, but with colored pencil work one can try to erase, but it NEVER completely goes away.

Yellow and Purple Orchid
colored pencil on black card stock
original - 9" x 12"

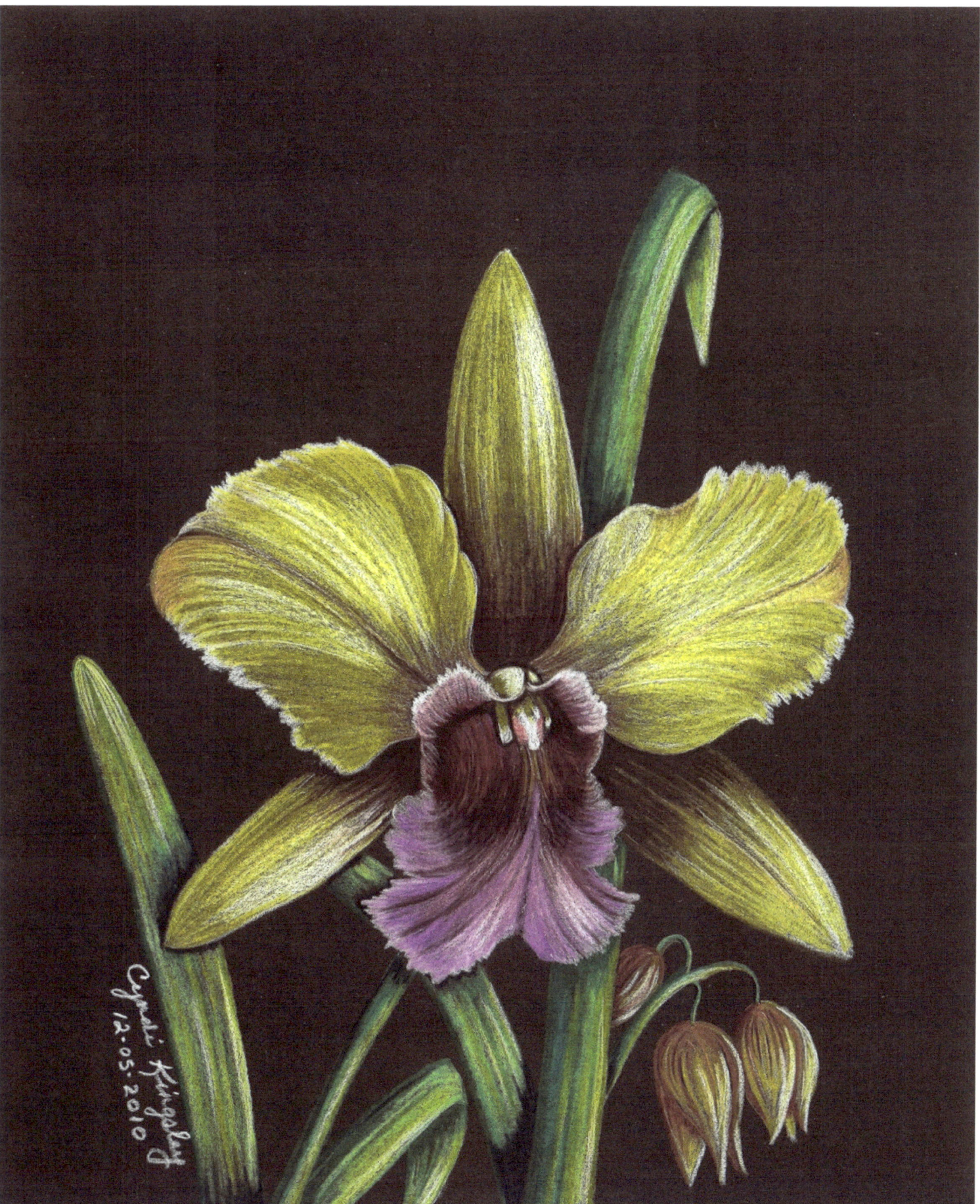

This is the third orchid I did with colored pencil. My daughter-in-law loved all three orchid works so much (and said so several times) that now they adorn the walls of her home.

Purple Orchid
colored pencil on black card stock
original- 9" x 12"

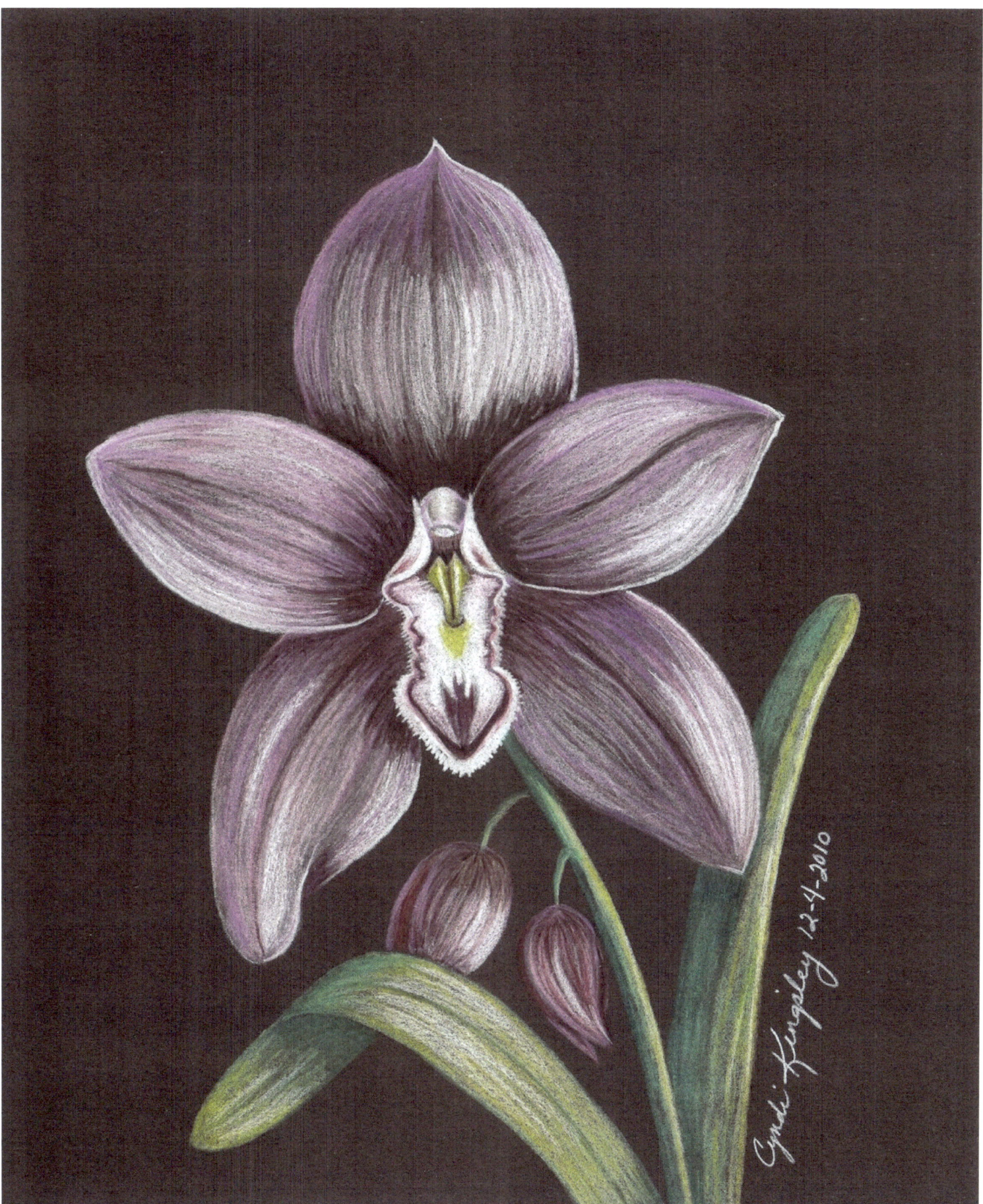

I love cameo pins and, at one time, I had a collection of them. I thought it would be a nice challenge for me to do a colored pencil work of a cameo. Making pearls shine with
colored pencil, definitely, took some thought, but I was happy with what I achieved.

Cameo Appearance
colored pencil on black card stock
original 9" x 12"

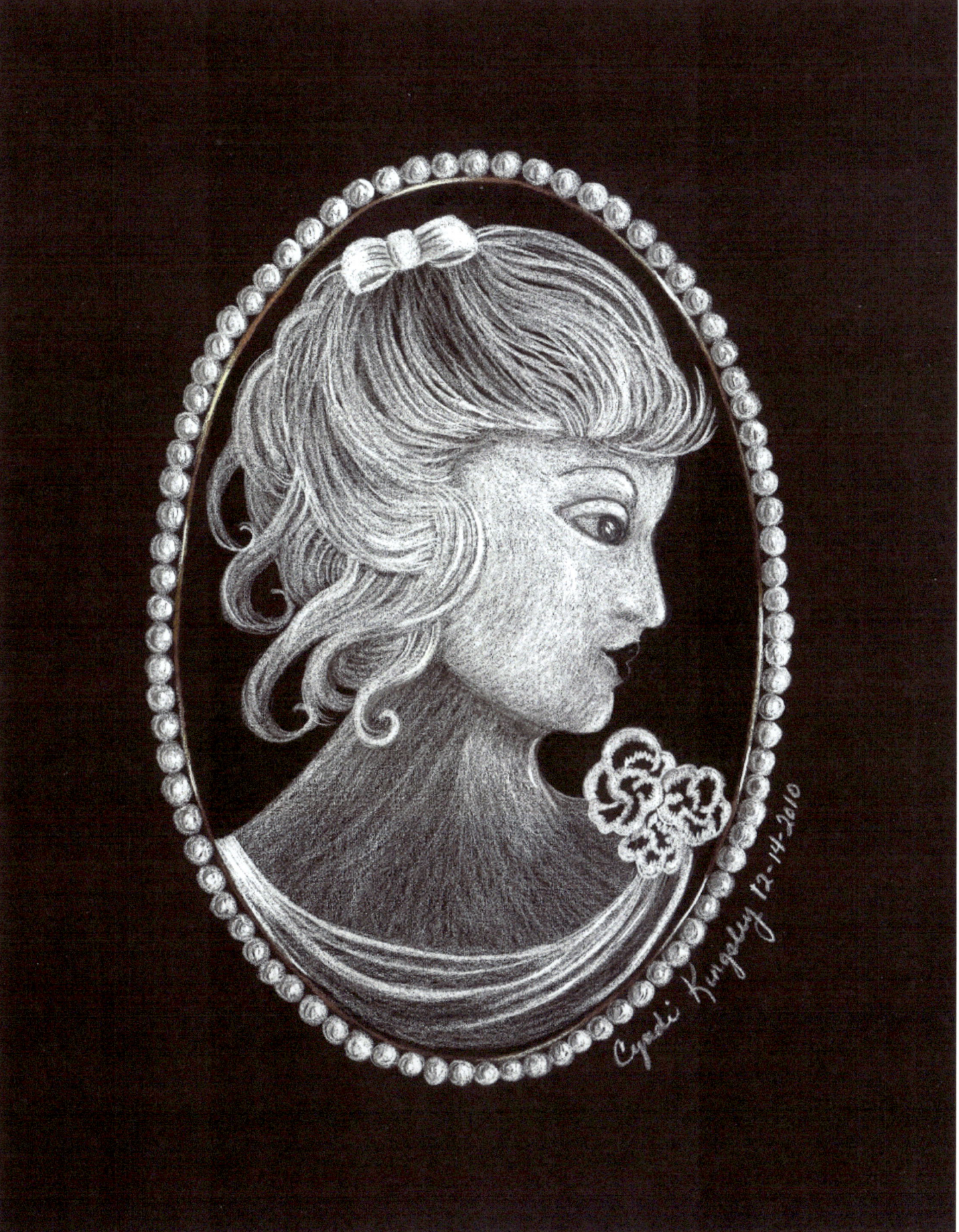

Blue Herons are such a graceful bird and I never get tired of watching them while I'm paddling in my kayak. I have painted several Blue Heron with acrylics, but this is the only one I've done (so far) with colored pencil.

Blue Heron On The Dock
colored pencil on bristol
original "9 x 12"

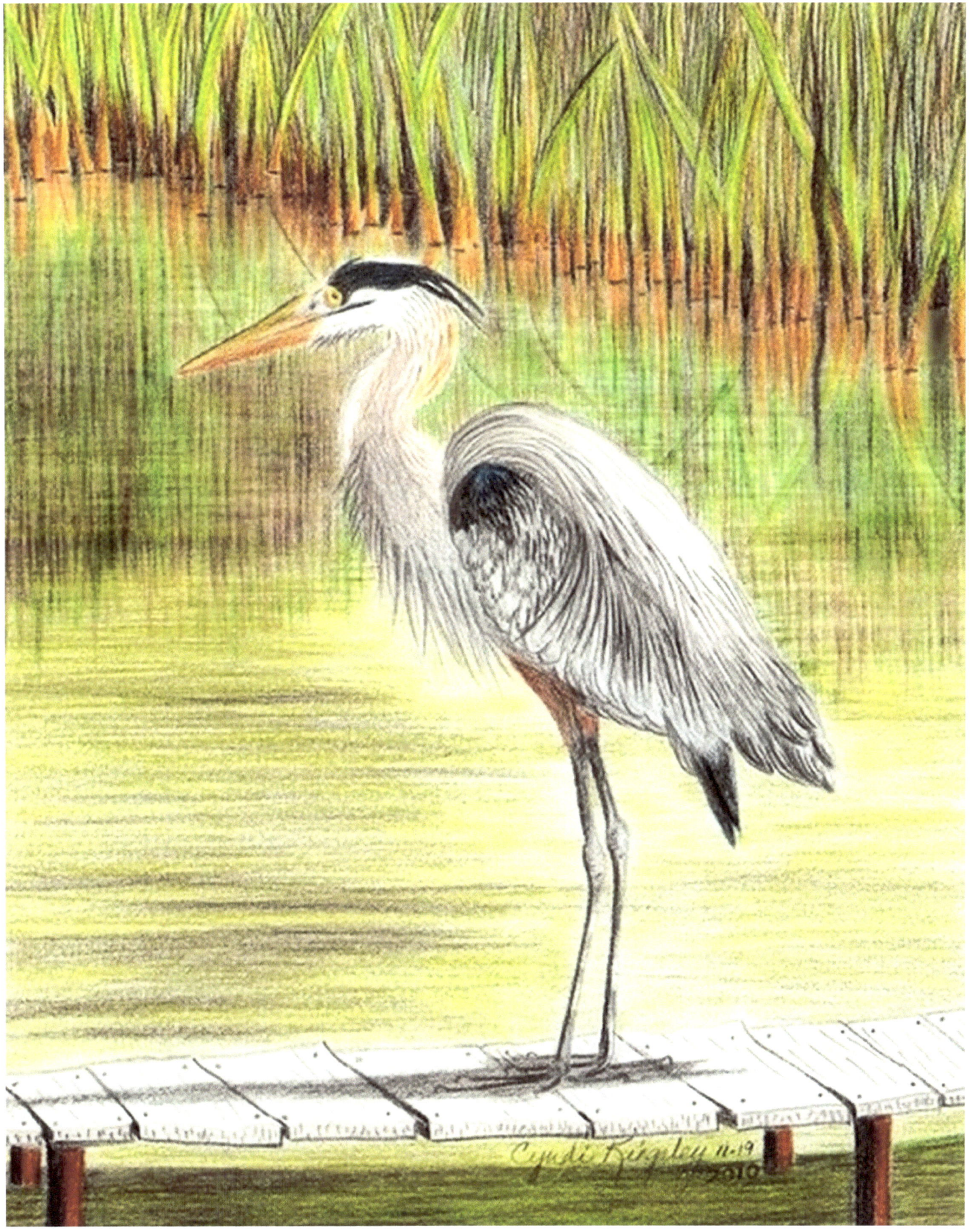

Cyndi Kingsley was born in Auburn, New York and was raised in Rochester, New York. As an adult, she has lived in various states across the USA.

While living in Erie, Pennsylvania (1998) she began painting with the intention to sell. She lived near a portion of Lake Erie where the shore was made up of smooth small rocks. Cyndi collected some of those rocks and began painting Christmas scenes on them. She drilled holes in them, ran a ribbon through them for hanging, and went to a seasonal farm market to see if they would be interested in buying her painted rocks. The owner loved them and bought them all. She then retailed them in her market. Cyndi continued to paint and sell rocks (in Erie) at an outside, local, touristy, flea market where vacationers, from all over the USA, and locals, frequented.

Cyndi now lives on the gulf side of Florida, and paints on canvas. She sells them outright or by commission.

www.ingramcontent.com/pod-product-compliance
Lightning Source LLC
Chambersburg PA
CBHW051824210526
45473CB00005B/1727